What Made Me
Love
My Profession

KRYSTAL PASILIAO

NEWMAN SPRINGS PUBLISHING
320 Broad Street
Red Bank, NJ 07701

First originally published by Newman Springs Publishing 2019

ISBN 978-1-64096-773-1 (Paperback)
ISBN 978-1-64531-423-3 (Hardcover)
ISBN 978-1-64096-774-8 (Digital)

Printed in the United States of America

My world is 24 inches in diameter as far as I can see—all one color: blue. It was the first time my feet ever left solid ground as I took to the air. I was leaving the smallest of islands and going to a new life—a life in the United States of America. I was glued to the window. My heart never quit racing in anticipation of the life that lay ahead. Only when the kind stewardess interrupted my racing thoughts to generously offer me something to drink did my thoughts pause. The flight seemed to take forever, but when we landed, it felt ever so short. We landed in Texas.

I had this feeling inside me that I could not hide. The frightened feeling of being alone in another country. To be in unfamiliar place with strangers and not knowing what to expect was very frightening to me. I started asking myself, "Will I love it here? Are the people nice? Will I like my job? Is the work hard?" It was not about to let these fears control me. I know that the best way to conquer them is to jump right in to get started with my new life. That's just what I did—thinking about this new job in a different country. It's the very first job I ever had away from home.

So that very first day I arrived, I was met at the airport by the supervisor of the hospital who hired me. She was holding a cardboard in front of her with my name and the hospital's name written on it. I approached her and we introduced ourselves. She was a lovely woman with a very pleasant personality. We talked in the car while she drove. While we were talking, I couldn't take my eyes off the breathtaking view of the countryside. It was so beautiful to look at. Everything was so green and peaceful. The wind was blowing on my face and hair, and I could smell the freshness of the air and the fragrance of the flowers and trees.

They had gorgeous houses, and I noticed some people were wearing cowboy outfits with hats and heavy-looking boots. They were riding horses also, just like in the movies.

What a wonderful feeling to be in another country and to be able to see such wondrous things that I would have never seen in my own country. We then reached our destination. She took me to an apartment where I would be staying with the other nurses. These nurses were from the same country where I came from. They came here through the same agency, but most of them had been living here for quite a long time now and were already professionals. They were very kind and friendly to me. I liked them the moment I met them. They made me feel comfortable and at home.

My roommates took me to the hospital where I will be working. They introduced me to everybody. They were awesome. The hospital was not so big and located in a small town of Houston, Texas. In fact, it was so small, everybody for the most part knew everyone.

Our apartment was just walking distance to the hospital, about 10 minutes away. The shops, the post office, and the banks were not far apart from each other and were all in walking distance. The stores were small, but they carry most everything you need from clothing to home and garden. They were like ma and pa shops.

Everything was moving along so fast. It was only my second day, and I was already in orientation. Just four quick weeks, and it was over. I had learned a lot, and I was beginning to enjoy my work. I was able to quickly adjust myself to a new environment and able to find my way around. The work was not really hard like what I had thought so.

In a large convention hall filled with hundreds of other hopeful nursing students, I sat to take the state boards. I had heard all the horror stories of others about the state boards being too grueling, much more comfortable with the American experience. The language, the nuisances—yet they failed the state boards. About 50 percent passing, but I passed.

I had never been so happy in my life.

I still had contact with my friends back home. Most of them had come to the States and were now working in Los Angeles, California. They would call me almost every night and try to convince me to move to LA so that we could all be together again. They convinced me after much prodding, and that I would love LA as much as I loved Texas and the Texans.

So after six months, I finally found myself in Los Angeles, California. I was so happy to see my friends again. They gave me a little welcome party. It felt like I was home, again.

Few days later, I started searching for a job. I found one through a nursing registry. It was not very long before the registry nurse recruiter and I became friends. She started sending me to different hospitals where they were in need of a registered nurse.

Everything was going great, not just in my professional life but my personal life as well. I went back home and got married to my boyfriend. I then came back to the States with my husband. My husband's family migrated to Hawaii at the same time. My sister's petition from her husband came, and she was finally able to join him. After a few years, she brought our parents here under permanent visas. We were finally all together in this country—our new home.

One year later, I landed a new job at a big hospital here in LA. I had been working a lot at this hospital, in emergency room. I was already familiar with their system, and I really liked and enjoyed working in their ER. I decided to join them and became one of their staff. People were warm and friendly. They had a team approach and were very organized. I worked the morning shift, 8 hours a day, full-time position. It was not unusual for me to stay for four more hours if they needed help on the second shift. It was hard at times, but I already got used to it. This is the kind of work I chose. I enjoyed doing it, and I already planned to continue working as an ER nurse at this hospital until I retire.

It was not unusual to be assigned three or four patients per nurse. One morning, I was given rooms 1, 2, and 3, each with one patient. I was walking to see my new patient in room 2 to start an IV and draw blood. My practice was to always check on my other patients and their monitors. As I walked by room 1, before going to room 2, I saw the patient was sleeping, but when I looked up at the cardiac monitor, I noticed the rhythm appeared to be reflecting myocardial infarction, which means that the patient was having a heart attack. I woke up the patient and asked her if she was having any chest pains or discomfort. She said no. I immediately did a 12-lead EKG to confirm my suspicion. The EKG indicated that she was having a heart attack. I hurriedly showed it to our ER doctor, who was caring for her. He then went to the patient's room and talked to her. He told her that she was having a heart attack in her sleep. She claimed that she was having chest pains in her dream but thought it was just a dream. The doctor told her that her nurse saved her life. That I was her "angel." We immediately gave her the thrombolytic therapy to prevent further damage to her heart. Then a cardiologist saw her for consult. I later transferred her to the Critical Care Unit, placing her in someone else's hands.

It was not unusual for our assignment to change, to rotate to another area of the emergency room. There was a time when I was assigned to be the advocate nurse. My job was to assess all patients checking in to see if they needed immediate care or if they could wait to be seen in their tum.

On one such afternoon, there was a Hispanic male in his twenties who had been brought in to our ER by his friend. He spoke Spanish only, but the friend translated for him. He said he just started itching all over like a few minutes ago. He could not remember what he ate or took prior to the itching. I looked at him. I could not see any hives or bumps on the face or arms, but he looked flushed. He was breathing okay. But when I took his blood pressure, it was 170/110. I asked him if he had any history of high blood pressure. His answer was no. I then repeated his blood pressure and it read 107/60. I immediately suspected he was going into anaphylactic shock—a severe, potentially fatal systemic allergic reaction. I rushed him inside in a wheelchair and told his friend, "We will explain it to you later. He just needs immediate attention," Inside the medical area, I put him in room 4 and called our ER doctor, who happened to be closed by. I told him the problem. While giving a report to the doctor, I hooked up the patient to the monitor and started an intravenous line. The doctor called another nurse to help and started ordering the emergency drugs, another intravenous line, and crash cart to be brought to the bedside. He was taken to CCU in an hour. In about 2 hours later, my co-nurse who took care of him said, "He expired in the CCU half an hour ago. They could not bring his blood pressure up despite all the drugs and IV fluids. It just kept going down." Our supervisor came to me and said they had found out that he ate some oysters that noon prior to the reaction. His wife came later that day, wanting to visit him. She only knew he checked in for the itching. Our supervisor was the one who sat with her and told her.

Everything always seemed to happen so fast in the ER. Sometimes it got crazy and very busy. It was my turn to triage. Our receptionist called my attention to the triage room. She told me that a friend of hers outside was having chest pains. I took him into the triage room and told him that I needed to run an EKG. I was asking him questions while preparing for the EKG. He said he had been having the burning sensation off and on in the middle of his chest since the day before. The EKG showed acute myocardial infarction. I did not waste any time. I pushed him in a gurney to the medical area and told the charge nurse to call the doctor. I put him in room 3. He had everything on—monitor and oxygen. He had an IV line. Aspirin and nitroglycerin were given. Now, he said, he was pain free. Chest x-ray was done. He was awaiting cardiology consult. I went back to triage. Every time I had to do something in the medical area, I always checked on him. He looked comfortable reading a newspaper and there was a family member with him. About half hour later, I saw the cardiologist going into room 3, bringing in the echocardiogram machine inside the room. Suddenly, the cardiologist appeared at the door. His right ankle was bleeding. It had been slashed by the ECHO machine's exposed metal edges. He went to the surgical area for our ER surgeon to suture him. That halted the patient's procedure because the doctor is now a patient. Meanwhile, the patient in room 3 waited at least another two hours to be seen by a now-injured cardiologist. By 3 pm that same day, our supervisor asked me to stay over until 7 pm. We were down one nurse. When I agreed to stay over, I was assigned to take over the patient in room 3 in the medical area. It was the same patient who had been in room 3 earlier that day. That outgoing nurse gave me report. It made me angry when she told me that she had not yet started the heparin drip (blood thinner) that was ordered hours ago at 10:30 am and it was now past 3 pm and the patient had not gotten that important drug, which was supposed to be the priority. I told her this patient was most acute at this moment. I couldn't do anything but hurriedly started the heparin drip. The doctor who was attending to this patient told me that this patient is going to telemetry per the cardiologist. I disagreed and questioned him. I told him that I was not comfortable taking him to telemetry, because we all knew that this patient, an acute MI, should be admitted to Critical Care Unit at least overnight. The doctor replied, "The cardiologist thinks that the patient is stable enough to go to telemetry. He's the one who makes the decision." I was so worried about this patient. I had this feeling that something was going to happen to him, that I needed to do something before it happens. First of all, my mind was telling me that he was not going to be safe in telemetry tonight. I had no choice but to get him a telemetry bed. Once his bed was assigned, accompanied by an EMT, we took him to the floor on portable cardiac monitor and oxygen. Upstairs on the floor, I noticed that his bed was by the window. It was the B-bed and you could hardly get by without pushing the A-bed with another patient in it to the other side of the room. The room was very small; it had two beds in one room. Almost too tight to get a gurney inside. This room was located at the end of the telemetry floor by the entrance coming out of the elevator. It was about 60 feet away from the nurses' station. But worse yet, there was no portable telemetry box available to hook up the patient. No way to monitor him from the nurses' station. I told the EMT who had accompanied me to go find a telemetry box while I watch the patient and his monitor because we were not leaving him in the room without a portable monitor. It was at least 15 to 20 minutes before they finally got him a monitor. I also spoke to the nurse in charge of the floor and insisted that he should be moved closer to the nurse's station as soon as possible. "This patient is an acute MI and needed close observation." She then replied, "Okay."

I was so tired when I got home that night. But my mind was still on that patient who had a heart attack. I was still worried about him, wondering why everything went so wrong for him from the very start.

The next day, as soon as I stepped in our emergency room, not even clocked in yet, I saw the doctor from the day before—Dr. White— standing at the entrance of the reception area. He appeared to be very eager to talk to me.

"I have bad news for you. The guy you took care of yesterday in room 3 with acute MI—he passed away last night at 10:30 pm with a massive MI. We couldn't revive him."

I was shocked and speechless. I felt like I wanted to cry. "See, Dr. White?" I said. "What did I tell you? He should have been in CCU at least one day to be safe. That's why I was not comfortable when I took him to the telemetry floor yesterday. I had the feeling something will happen to him."

"I know," he said. "I should have said something to the cardiologist. I should have disagreed with him." I saw in Dr. White's face that he felt sorry for the patient too, but it's too late now. He was already gone. I had tried everything to save that gentleman, but it seemed like everything went the other way. For what reason, I'll never knew.

Months passed by, our emergency room was under construction. I called in a young woman in the triage room. She was about 32 years old, very petite, well dressed, very anxious, and complaining of chest tightness not going away, which started while she was driving on her way to work that morning. She denied other symptoms. I quickly did her EKG without asking any questions, yet not even taking her vital signs. The EKG showed she was having a heart attack. I immediately put her in the wheelchair and rushed her inside. I showed her EKG to our ER doctor and right away she was given the emergency drugs for heart attack and was admitted to the CCU.

Our emergency room had been very busy; almost like a trauma center, or it could be worst. This time we had two RNs in the triage area. Our registration lobby was packed. I noticed an old woman in her sixties waiting in a wheelchair. According to our front desk receptionist, her caregiver dropped her off and disappeared. I then brought her to the triage room. I asked her why she thinks the caregiver brought her to the hospital. She said they told her that she was not breathing that good. She claimed that her breathing was fine, but they would not believe her. She denied having other symptoms like chest pain, etc. I checked her vital signs, oxygen saturation, lung sounds, and EKG. They were okay but not excellent. I called the charge nurse to give me a bed for her, but I was told that she has to wait for a little bit more because it was very saturated and crazy inside, but she will be next to get inside. So I let the patient know, and we will get her in as soon as they have a bed. Patients kept pouring in that day nonstop. We had been closed to saturation, and our triage was endless. But this old lady in the wheelchair caught my attention. Why have they not brought her in yet? It has been a while she waited. I quickly called the charge nurse again. She said that a room is now being cleaned for her. I took her inside and asked one of our EMT's to help me put her in the bed, because she was very heavy and helpless. While we were putting her on the cardiac monitor, she became unresponsive and her monitor showed ventricular fibrillation. I called a code blue and started CPR on her and the EMT started bagging her. Everybody came to help, and we were able to revive her and she made it to the CCU.

There were times when our emergency department was quiet in the morning hours when we came in at 0700. Paramedics and ambulances come through the back door when they bring in their patients. One time they brought us an alcoholic. The paramedic report said the patient probably fell due to intoxication. "He had been complaining of upper back pain ever since we picked him up on the street." The man appeared to be in some discomfort. Moaning and groaning, he was very loud and restless—very typical characteristics of an alcohol abuse. You can smell the alcohol from his breath even from the distance and his skin was flushed. He was very intoxicated but awake and alert and able to answer questions. He claimed that he did not fall. I put him in a room and my mind was telling me that this man, whether he is alcoholic or not, was having a cardiac problem. I immediately did an EKG on him. My guess was right. His

EKG revealed an acute myocardial infarction, which means that he was having a heart attack. Our ED doctor immediately ordered the emergency drugs and put him in the hospital, to the CCU.

Sometimes I get to work on the surgical side of our emergency room where I enjoy working most. One morning, when I came on at 0700 in the surgical area, the outgoing night shift gave me report on a patient in trauma room 10. The report was this patient was a diabetic elderly lady came in last night with a gangrenous foot. Now she was awaiting a podiatry consult for possible left foot amputation. Nothing else was ordered, which means that nothing was done on her all night. No pain medication was given. No labs or IV fluids were ordered either. She was on nothing by mouth only until she sees the podiatrist on call in the morning. I went to check on the patient. She appeared very uncomfortable, freezing, and in a lot of pain. She was still wearing her house clothes and no blanket. She was moaning and grimacing. Her left foot was hanging on the side of the bed, skin very dark, cold and draining some fluids. No dressing. I introduced myself to her and explained to her what she was waiting for. I promised to come back for her pain medicine. I first put a hospital gown on her and gave her a warm blanket. I covered her left foot with a dressing and took a pillow and elevated her foot. Then I took her blood sugar and put her on the monitor for her vital signs. I promised her I will come back for her pain medicine. When I went back to the nurse's station, I saw our ER doctor assigned to her for the morning shift and it happened to be the chief of our ED. I asked her if she can order a pain medicine for this patient in trauma 10. After I medicated the patient for pain, I talked to our chief about the doctor who took care of this patient in trauma 10 last night. He was a moonlighter, a noncaring doctor. He let the patient suffer all night. No pain med ordered. No labs. No IV fluid. Patient was diabetic and on nothing by mouth all night. He ignored the patient's grimacing. I also reported the night-shift nurse to our supervisor about the same thing. After our chief heard everything, she reassured me that she will take care of it and said, "Don't worry." The next morning, I was again assigned in the surgical area. Our chief saw me and talked to me. She said that the moonlighter doctor who took care of the patient in trauma 10 "is not coming back anymore because I fired him."

I said, "Thanks, Doc. The patient did not deserve to be treated like that. She had suffered enough already."

Our hospital, being the closest and very visible to the freeway, frequently gets a lot of drop-offs. One time, a taxi driver brought us a full-term pregnant woman who was having a baby in the taxi back seat. Another time, a man was dropped off by someone and left dying on the ambulance entrance, bleeding with gunshot wounds. Sometimes they would just run inside our emergency room with stab wounds and pass out with blood all over the floor. They still made it. We had no deaths from stab wounds or gunshot wounds yet because we had the best surgeons in our ED. I was very proud of them. They were very experienced and fast.

We sometimes get young people coming in through the back door. This young woman, about thirteen years old, was running inside and screaming. She was by herself. She was saying that she had a baby. We could not see any baby in her arms and since she was wearing tight blue jeans we could not tell. When we got close to her, we saw her pants saturated with blood. We then took her pants off and saw a tiny premature baby hanging on the side of her leg and not breathing. The baby was dead. With permission, we called her family and the social worker. We also blessed the baby, gave him a name, and did the routine post-mortem care.

Again we had a paramedic run, brought in to our ER, a full-term pregnant woman—her first baby and first pregnancy—was in labor. Her husband was with them. I called the Labor and Delivery that we were coming up with this patient. I took the patient to L&D in a gurney with the help of our EMT. Her husband came along. Upstairs in L&D, no one was there. No one was at the nurses' station. No patients in the rooms. The whole place was empty. They knew we were coming because I called from the ER. We kept shouting and calling everybody but no one answered and nobody was coming out. "Where is everybody?" The patient was already bearing down and could not hold on. So I told my coworker EMT to grab any clean cloth and baby's suction bulb from one of the rooms just in case. I saw the baby's head almost out. A few minutes later, I delivered the baby. The baby started crying. It was a healthy baby boy and in no distress. All of a sudden, the Labor and Delivery staff came out from nowhere when they heard a baby cry. The patient's husband was so mad. He started cursing, but I managed to calm him down. I congratulated him and told him to enjoy the moment. Take pictures of his baby and wife. He thanked us before we left. I later made an incident report.

Back to the emergency room. When I was walking toward the front door with our ward clerk, a woman was crying outside the door of room 5 saying that her baby was not breathing. We went inside the room and checked on the baby. He was not breathing and the pulse was very faint. I told the clerk to call code blue. I gave the baby ventilations by using the ambu bag. When the clerk came back, she did the ventilations and I did the chest compressions. Help came right away. I was able to get a line on the baby with no difficulty. I was so thankful. We immediately gave her all emergency drugs through intravenous line. The baby survived. We then took her to the neonatal CCU in stable condition. One morning, it was change of shift, and I was getting report from the night-shift staff about a patient in room 11. She reported that this patient is an alcoholic brought in by paramedics. He was very intoxicated. Very loud and restless. She said that they had given him all the drugs for his intoxication and restlessness but still the same, and he was trying to climb out of bed. The side rails were up. They tied him down, but he was able to untie himself. He had been yelling all night long and banging the rails. Sometimes he will go to sleep, but most of the time he was wide awake. They did all the blood tests, including alcohol and drug screen. He was on intravenous fluids with vitamins continuously. When the blood tests came back, he was positive on almost everything. He will be reevaluated by the doctor in the morning. It was almost 0800 after I did my nursing assessments and vital signs on this patient. Our ER doctor came to check on him. I asked him if we could order head CT on this patient because everything was ordered last night, but I did not see a CT scan of head ordered. "If you don't mind," I asked the doctor. He responded, "Go ahead, order it." I right away ordered the CT scan of head and then I called the nuclear tech and said to him stat and that the patient is ready. Within seven minutes, they came and took the patient to CT. It did not take that long. The tech came back with the patient, and the radiologist called our ER doctor for the result of the CT. He said it showed a bleed in the head. Right away our ER doctor ordered me to prepare the patient for transfer to our other hospital that specializes on neurosurgery. I then immediately moved fast and prepared the patient. I gave a report to the accepting hospital and called Critical Care Transport. Within an hour the patient was transferred to another hospital for his neurosurgery. I hoped he will make it.

I like working in triage room because here you get to see and talk to a lot of people, sick or not. I like to help sick people, and I like to be in a crowd. In triage most of the time there is a long line of people checking in. We carefully assess and prioritize care according to acuity and need of people. We provide immediate care and treatment in the waiting room lobby based on our ER protocol whenever possible.

There was this thirteen-year-old female brought in by her mother to the triage room. She appeared to be in some discomfort, bent over, complaining of severe abdominal pain that started few hours ago. Denied other symptoms. When I asked her for last menstrual period, her mother got upset and told me that there is no way her daughter is pregnant. "That I better not! Think of that," she told me. She even added that she makes sure of that because she keeps track of her daughter's menstrual cycle and she just got her period recently. I then asked the patient to lie down in the bed so I can palpate where exactly her pain is. When she pointed to me the location of her pain, I suddenly felt the head of the fetus in the right upper quadrant of her abdomen when she was having contractions. I told her mother, "I am pretty sure that she is pregnant. So I am going to page our GYN doctor on call." I spoke to our GYN doctor and told him about the patient. In less than fifteen minutes, he came down and saw the patient. He told the mother that her daughter is pregnant and in labor. That her pain is labor pain or contractions. The doctor then asked me to help him push the patient in the gurney to Labor and Delivery.

Two hours later, the doctor called me in the ED to tell me that the patient had a baby girl and weighed 5 lbs and they were both okay.

One morning, I was getting ready to call another patient, when a middle-aged woman was screaming, pulling her six-year-old daughter inside with her. She stated her daughter cannot "pee-pee." I then put them in a room and asked the mother since when was she having this problem—

unable to urinate. She said since Sunday morning. She also stated that they were seen in pediatric clinic that same day. They did a urine test, which came back normal, and they were sent home. The mother was crying and in panic, but the little patient was so quiet and calm. She was just listening. She did not appear to be in distress. I calmly asked the patient to lie down and to let me take a look at her vagina to see why she cannot "peepee." When I separated her legs, I saw a lot of redness, swelling, and rashes around her vagina down to both inner thighs. It appeared to be herpes. There were marks of fingers down below her inner thighs. I suspected right away that this child had been molested. I told the mother that her daughter will be seen by a pediatrician and by a gynecologist who is specialized in the female part. I then called both doctors on call on the phone and told them what I had seen and suspected. They both came down right away. They examined the patient and talked to the mother. At the same time, I contacted the social worker and notified the police. After all the interviews and investigations by the doctors, social worker, and the police, we had found out that the patient's stepfather had been molesting her at night while her mother was at work. The mother kept crying and was refusing to file charges against her boyfriend. She said he had been giving her money for support. Not only that, their story got more complicated when the mother's sister and her three-year-old daughter walked in to the emergency room to visit them. The sister admitted to the social worker and police that she and her three-year-old daughter too had been molested by the same man at night while her sister goes to work. That same time we had a call from the other police that they had found the stepfather at home and they already took him to jail. The six-year-old patient as well as the three-year-old child of the sister of the mother were in the social worker's custody for the time being while awaiting the hearing.

It was one of those craziest days we had in the emergency room. It was so busy and full of crazy people too. Some were fighting trying to get to the front line to check in. Some were getting irate complaining about the wait time. Others were arguing for no reason just to get attention. This was our old emergency room. It was so small. There was not enough room or beds to accommodate a lot of people inside. A lot of times we were closed to saturation. But paramedics still come in and kept bringing in patients through the back door. They would say everybody is closed too. They occupied the beds so we could not bring in any more patients from the front lobby. There was nowhere to put anybody.

I got a call in the triage room from our charge nurse. She was sending me an employee from the lab to the lobby to be triaged first. She said he had been vomiting and complaining of abdominal pain. She added that there was not a single bed available to put him. Meanwhile she wanted me to triage him first and then to bring him back while she makes a bed for him. The lab employee came out to the lobby by himself, walking, sweating a lot, and appeared to be in distress. I immediately put him in the gurney and told him that I will do an EKG quick. I had a feeling I told him that it looked like it was his heart and not his stomach. The EKG showed he was having a heart attack. I told the front desk to call to the back that I was coming in with the patient and need a bed stat. I rushed him back inside in a gurney. We were almost flying. We made him a room while they were moving the other patients around. He was immediately given the emergency cardiac medications and then transported to the CCU.

One morning, I was getting ready to start my shift at 0700 when I received report from the outgoing night shift. There was a woman in her late seventies leaning on the glass door right at the front entrance, who appeared to be in some distress. Because she was unable to walk any farther, I grabbed a wheelchair and offered it to her. She said she drove her car all the way to the fifth floor parking lot and parked there because the parking lot was full. She then took